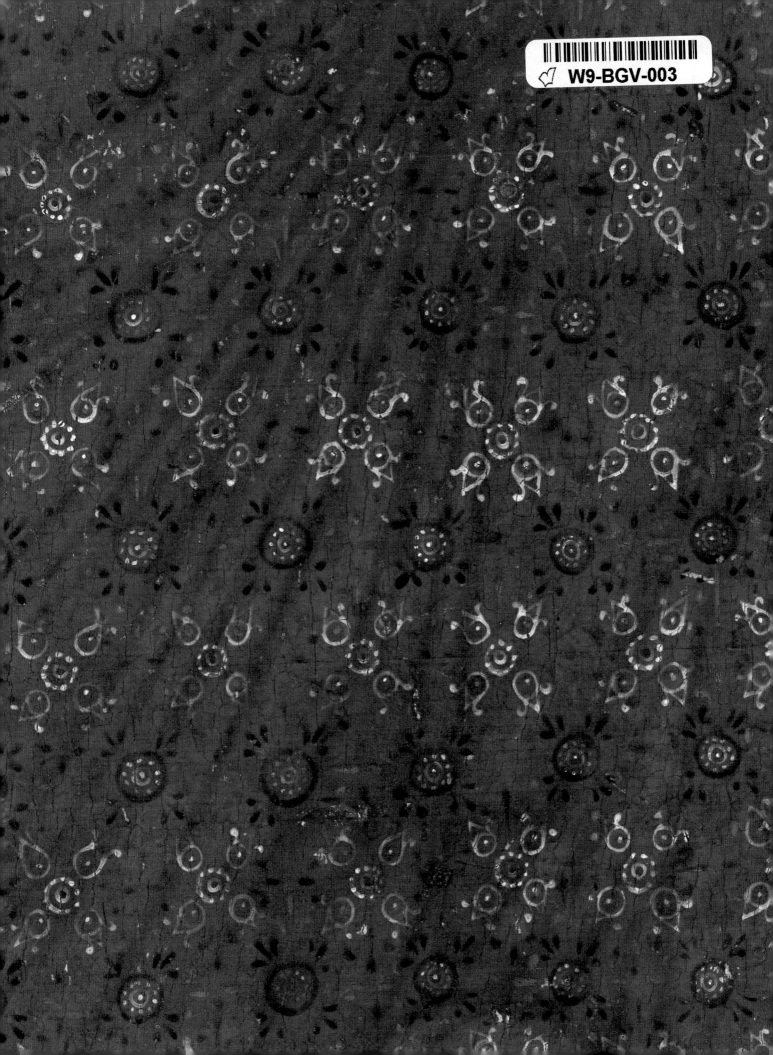

Carols for Christmas

Hark! The Herald Angels Sing

Music arranged by Barrie Carson Turner

THE NATIONAL GALLERY, LONDON

Frances Lincoln
in association with
National Gallery Publications, London

Angels, from the Realms of Glory

French traditional

3. Sages, leave your contemplations;
    Brighter visions beam afar;
    Seek the great Desire of Nations;
    Ye have seen his natal star:
        Come and worship...

4. Though an infant now we view him,
    He shall fill his Father's throne,
    Gather all the nations round him,
    Every knee shall then bow down:
        Come and worship...

In the Bleak Midwinter

Gustav Holst (1874-1934)
Words by Christina Georgina Rossetti
(1830-94)

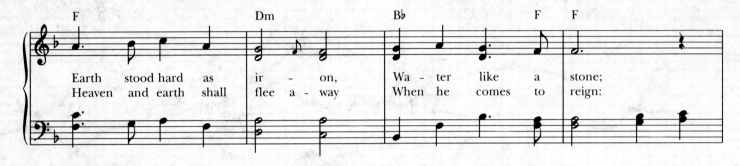

3. Angels and archangels
May have gathered there,
Cherubim and seraphim
Thronged the air;
But only his mother
In her maiden bliss
Worshipped the Belovèd
With a kiss.

4. What can I give him,
Poor as I am?
If I were a shepherd
I would bring a lamb;
If I were a wise man
I would do my part
Yet what I can I give him –
Give my heart.

The First Nowell

English melody arr. John Stainer (1840-1901)
Words traditional

1. The first Nowell the angel did say Was to
2. They lookèd up and saw a star Shining

certain poor shepherds in fields as they lay; In fields where
in the east, beyond them far; And to the

they lay keeping their sheep, On a cold winter's night that
earth it gave great light, And so it continued both

was so deep: } *Now - ell, Now - ell, Now - ell, Now -*
day and night: }

ell, Born is the King of Is - ra - el.

3. And by the light of that same star,
   Three Wise Men came from country far;
   To seek for a king was their intent,
   And to follow the star wherever it went:
   Nowell, Nowell, Nowell, Nowell…

4. This star drew nigh unto the north-west;
   O'er Bethlehem it took its rest,
   And there it did both stop and stay,
   Right over the place where Jesus lay:
   Nowell, Nowell, Nowell, Nowell…

5. Then entered in those Wise Men three,
   Fell reverently upon their knee,
   And offered there, in his presence,
   Their gold and myrrh and frankincense:
   Nowell, Nowell, Nowell, Nowell…

6. Then let us all with one accord
   Sing praises to our heavenly Lord,
   That hath made heaven and earth of nought,
   And with his blood mankind hath bought:
   Nowell, Nowell, Nowell, Nowell…

Silent Night

Franz Grüber (1787-1863)
Original German words by
Joseph Mohr (1792-1848)
Translation anon.

2. Silent night, holy night,
   Shepherds first saw the light,
   Heard resounding clear and long,
   Far and near, the angel song:
   Christ the Saviour is here,
   Christ the Saviour is here.

3. Silent night, holy night,
   Son of God, oh, how bright
   Love is smiling from thy face,
   Peals for us the hour of grace.
   Christ our Saviour is born,
   Christ our Saviour is born.

O Come, All Ye Faithful

John Francis Wade (1711-86)
Words 18th century

At a moderate pace

1. O come, all ye faith - ful, Joy - ful and tri - um - phant, O come ye, O come ye to Beth - le - hem; Come and be - hold him, Born the King of An - gels: O come, let us a - dore him, O come, let us a - dore him, O come, let us a - dore him, Christ the Lord.

2. God of God, Light of Light, Lo! he ab - hors not the Vir - gin's womb; Ve - ry God, Be - got - ten, not cre - a - ted:

3. Sing, choirs of angels,
Sing in exultation.
Sing, all ye citizens of heaven above;
Glory to God
In the highest:
    O come, let us adore him…

4. Yea, Lord, we greet thee,
Born this happy morning,
Jesu, to thee be glory given;
Word of the Father,
Now in flesh appearing:
    O come, let us adore him…

The Holly and the Ivy

English traditional

At a moderate pace

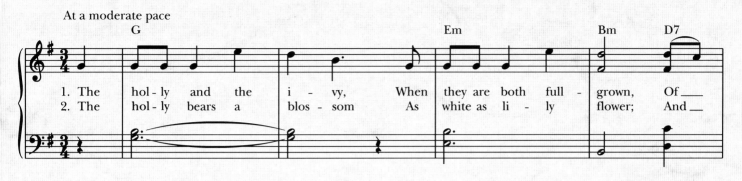

1. The hol-ly and the i - vy, When they are both full - grown, Of ___
2. The hol-ly bears a blos - som As white as li - ly flower; And ___

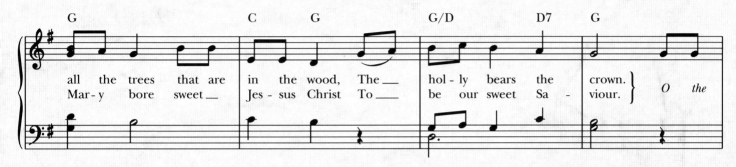

all the trees that are in the wood, The ___ hol-ly bears the crown.
Mar - y bore sweet ___ Jes - sus Christ To ___ be our sweet Sa - viour.

O the

ris - ing of the sun, ___ And the run - ning of the deer, The ___

play - ing of the mer - ry or - gan, Sweet sing - ing in the choir.

3. The holly bears a berry,
   As red as any blood;
   And Mary bore sweet Jesus Christ
   To do poor sinners good.
   O the rising of the sun…

4. The holly bears a prickle,
   As sharp as any thorn;
   And Mary bore sweet Jesus Christ
   On Christmas Day in the morn.
   O the rising of the sun…

5. The holly bears a bark,
   As bitter as any gall;
   And Mary bore sweet Jesus Christ,
   For to redeem us all.
   O the rising of the sun…

Hark! The Herald Angels Sing

Felix Mendelssohn (1809-47)
*from **Festgesang** (1840)*

1. Hark! The her - ald an - gels sing _____ Glor - y to the new - born King;
2. Christ, by high - est heaven a - dored, _____ Christ, the ev - er - last - ing Lord;

Peace on earth, and mer - cy mild, _____ God and sin - ners re - con - ciled.
Late in time be - hold him come, _____ Off - spring of a Vir - gin's womb.

Joy - ful, all you na - tions, rise, _____ Join the tri - umph of the skies; _____
Veiled in flesh the God - head see; _____ Hail, the In - car - nate De - it - y, _____

With the an-gel-lic hosts pro-claim, Christ is ___ born in Beth - le - hem.
Pleased as man with man to dwell, Je - sus, ___ our Em - man - u - el!

Hark! The her - ald an - gels sing, Glo - ry ___ to the new - born King.

3. Hail the heaven-born Prince of Peace!
Hail the Sun of Righteousness!
Light and life to all he brings,
Risen with healing in his wings.
Mild he lays his glory by,
Born that man no more may die,
Born to raise the sons of earth,
Born to give them second birth.
Hark! The herald angels sing,
Glory to the new-born King.

Once in Royal David's City

Henry John Gauntlett (1805-76)
Words by Cecil Frances Alexander
(1818-95)

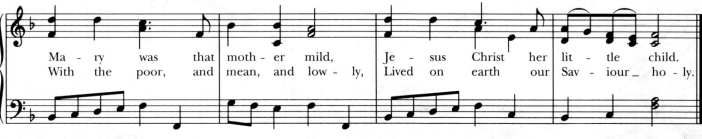

3. And through all his wondrous childhood
   He would honour and obey,
   Love and watch the lowly maiden,
   In whose gentle arms he lay.
   Christian children all must be
   Mild, obedient, good as he.

4. And our eyes at last shall see him,
   Through his own redeeming love,
   For that child so dear and gentle
   Is our Lord in heaven above;
   And he leads his children on
   To the place where he is gone.

God Rest You Merry, Gentlemen

English traditional

1. God rest you merry, gentlemen, Let nothing you dis-
2. From God our heavenly Father A blessèd angel

may, For Jesus Christ our Saviour Was born on Christmas
came, And unto certain shepherds Brought tidings of the

Day; To save us all from Satan's power When we were gone a-
same, That there was born in Bethlehem The Son of God by

stray: } O____ tidings of comfort and joy, Comfort and
name: }

joy; O____ tidings of comfort and joy.

3. 'Fear not,' then said the Angel,
   'Let nothing you affright,
   This day is born a Saviour
   Of virtue, power and might;
   So frequently to vanquish all
   The friends of Satan quite':
   O tidings of comfort and joy…

4. The shepherds at these tidings,
   Rejoicèd much in mind,
   And left their flocks a-feeding
   In tempest, storm, and wind,
   And went to Bethlehem straightway
   This blessèd babe to find:
   O tidings of comfort and joy…

5. And when they came to Bethlehem
   Where our sweet Saviour lay,
   They found him in a manger,
   Where oxen feed on hay;
   His mother Mary kneeling,
   Unto the Lord did pray:
   O tidings of comfort and joy…

6. Now to the Lord sing praises,
   All you within this place,
   And with true love and brotherhood
   Each other now embrace;
   This holy tide of Christmas
   All others doth deface:
   O tidings of comfort and joy…

O Little Town of Bethlehem

English traditional

3. How silently, how silently,
    The wondrous gift is given!
    So God imparts to human hearts
    The blessings of his heaven.
    No ear may hear his coming;
    But in this world of sin,
    Where meek souls will receive him, still
    The dear Christ enters in.

4. O holy Child of Bethlehem,
    Descend to us, we pray;
    Cast out our sin, and enter in,
    Be born in us today.
    We hear the Christmas angels
    The great glad tidings tell:
    O come to us, abide with us,
    Our Lord Emmanuel.

See Amid the Winter's Snow

John Goss (1800-1880)
Words by Edward Caswall
(1814-78)

1. See a-mid the win-ter's snow,
Born for us on earth be-low;
See the ten-der Lamb ap-pears,
Prom-ised from e-ter-nal years.

2. Lo, with-in a man-ger lies,
He who built the star-ry skies;
He who, throned in height sub-lime,
Sits a-mid the cher-u-bim.

Hail! thou ev-er bless-èd morn!
Hail, re-demp-tion's hap-py dawn!
Sing through all Je-ru-sa-lem,
Christ is born in Beth-le-hem.

3. Say, ye holy shepherds, say,
What your joyful news today;
Wherefore have ye left your sheep
On the lonely mountain steep?
Hail! thou ever-blessèd morn…

4. 'As we watched at dead of night,
Lo, we saw a wondrous light;
Angels singing "Peace on Earth",
Told us of the Saviour's birth.'
Hail! thou ever-blessèd morn…

5. Sacred Infant, all divine,
What a tender love was thine;
Thus to come from highest bliss
Down to such a world as this!
Hail! thou ever-blessèd morn…

6. Teach, O teach us, Holy Child,
By thy face so meek and mild;
Teach us to resemble thee
In thy sweet humility.
Hail! thou ever-blessèd morn…

Good King Wenceslas

*Melody from **Piae Cantiones** (1582)*
Words by J. M. Neale (1818-66)

1. Good King Wen - ces - las looked out On the Feast of Ste - phen,
2. 'Hith - er, page, and stand by me, If thou knowst it, tell - ing,

When the snow lay round a - bout, Deep and crisp and e - ven:
Yon - der pea - sant, who is he? Where and what his dwell - ing?'

Bright-ly shone the moon that night, Though the frost was cru - el, When a poor man
'Sire, he lives a good league hence, Un - der - neath the moun - tain, Right a - gainst the

came in sight, Gath - ering win - ter fu - el.
for - est fence, By Saint Ag - nes foun - tain.'

3. 'Bring me flesh and bring me wine,
   Bring me pine-logs hither:
   Thou and I will see him dine
   When we bear them thither.'
   Page and monarch, forth they went,
   Forth they went together;
   Through the rude wind's wild lament
   And the bitter weather.

4. 'Sire, the night is darker now,
   And the wind grows stronger;
   Fails my heart, I know not how;
   I can go no longer.'
   'Mark my footsteps, good my page;
   Tread thou in them boldly:
   Thou shalt find the winter's rage
   Freeze thy blood less coldly.'

5. In his master's steps he trod,
   Where the snow lay dinted;
   Heat was in the very sod
   Which the Saint had printed.
   Therefore, Christian men, be sure,
   Wealth or rank possessing,
   Ye who now will bless the poor,
   Shall yourselves find blessing.

Away in a Manger

William James Kirkpatrick (1838-1921)
Words anon.

2. The cattle are lowing, the baby awakes,
   But little Lord Jesus, no crying he makes.
   I love thee, Lord Jesus! Look down from the sky,
   And stay by my side until morning is nigh.

3. Be near me, Lord Jesus; I ask thee to stay
   Close by me for ever, and love me, I pray.
   Bless all the dear children in thy tender care,
   And fit us for heaven, to live with thee there.

30

While Shepherds Watched

Este's ***Psalmes*** *(1592)*

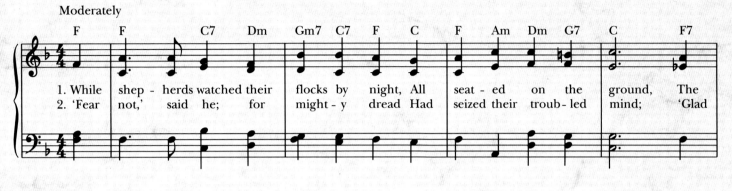

1. While shep-herds watched their flocks by night, All seat-ed on the ground, The
2. 'Fear not,' said he; for might-y dread Had seized their troub-led mind; 'Glad

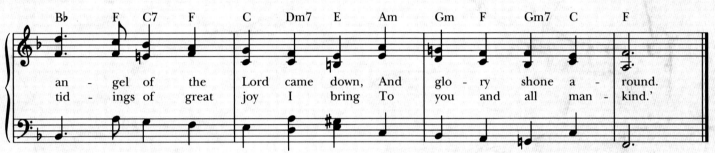

an-gel of the Lord came down, And glo-ry shone a-round.
tid-ings of great joy I bring To you and all man-kind.'

3. 'To you in David's town this day
   Is born of David's line
   A Saviour, who is Christ the Lord;
   And this shall be the sign:

4. 'The heavenly Babe you there shall find
   To human view displayed,
   All meanly wrapped in swaddling bands,
   And in a manger laid.'

5. Thus spake the seraph; and forthwith
   Appeared a shining throng
   Of angels praising God, who thus
   Addressed their joyful song:

6. 'All glory be to God on high,
   And to the earth be peace;
   Goodwill henceforth from heaven to men
   Begin and never cease!'

We Three Kings

Words and music by
John Henry Hopkins (1820-91)

Smooth and flowing

1. We three Kings of O - ri - ent are; Bear - ing gifts we trav - erse a - far,
2. Born a King on Beth-le - hem plain, Gold I bring, to crown him a - gain,

Field and foun - tain, moor and moun - tain, Fol - low-ing yon - der star:
King for - ev - er, ceas - ing nev - er, Ov - er us all to reign:

O ——

star of won - der, star of night, Star with roy - al beau - ty bright,

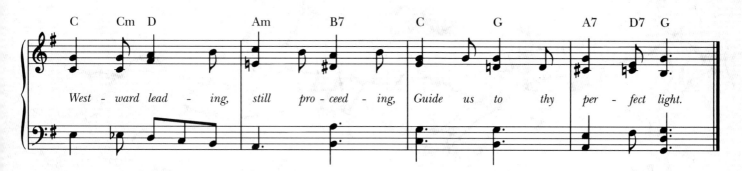

West - ward lead - ing, still pro - ceed - ing, Guide us to thy per - fect light.

3. Frankincense to offer have I,
   Incense owns a Deity nigh;
   Prayer and praising, all men raising,
   Worship him, God most high:
      O star of wonder, star of night…

4. Myrrh is mine, its bitter perfume
   Breathes a life of gathering gloom;
   Sorrowing, sighing, bleeding, dying,
   Sealed in the stone-cold tomb:
      O star of wonder, star of night…

5. Glorious now behold him arise,
   King and God and sacrifice!
   Heaven sings alleluia,
   Alleluia the earth replies:
      O star of wonder, star of night…

35

Deck the Hall

Welsh traditional

Brightly

1. Deck the hall with boughs of hol - ly, *Fa la la la la, la la la la,*
2. See the blaz - ing Yule be - fore us, *Fa la la la la, la la la la,*

'Tis the sea - son to be jol - ly, *Fa la la la la, la la la la,*
Strike the harp and join the chor - us, *Fa la la la la, la la la la,*

Don we now our gay ap - pa - rel, *Fa la la, la la la, la la la,*
Fol - low me in mer - ry mea - sure, *Fa la la, la la la, la la la,*

Troll the an - cient Yule - tide car - ol, *Fa la la la la, la la la la.*
While I tell of Yule - tide trea - sure, *Fa la la la la, la la la la.*

3. Fast away the old year passes,
   Fa la la la la, la la la la,
   Hail the new, ye lads and lasses,
   Fa la la la la, la la la la,
   Sing we joyous all together,
   Fa la la, la la la, la la la,
   Heedless of the wind and weather,
   Fa la la la la, la la la la.

O Christmas Tree

German traditional

2. O Christmas tree, O Christmas tree!
Thou hast a wondrous message.
O Christmas tree, O Christmas tree!
Thou hast a wondrous message.
Thou dost proclaim the Saviour's birth,
Goodwill to men and peace on earth.
O Christmas tree, O Christmas tree
Thou hast a wondrous message.

We Wish You a Merry Christmas

West Country traditional

2. We all want some figgy pudding,
   We all want some figgy pudding,
   We all want some figgy pudding,
   So bring some out here!
   Good tidings we bring…

3. We won't go until we get some,
   We won't go until we get some,
   We won't go until we get some,
   So bring some right here!
   Good tidings we bring…

Index

Page 11

The Nativity and the Annunciation
Jacopo di Cione
(active about 1362; died 1398/1400)
This is the first of a series of panels showing the life of Christ. Here the artist combines two scenes: above, the angel announces the birth of Christ to two astonished shepherds, while below is the scene of the Nativity.

Page 13

The Nativity, at Night
Ascribed to Geertgen tot Sint Jans
(around 1455/65-85/95)
Geertgen's use of dramatic light was exceptional for his time. Here the night is lit both by the Infant and by the angel in the background who casts light over the shepherd and flock.

Page 15

'Mystic Nativity'
Sandro Botticelli
(active by 1470-1510)
In Botticelli's unconventional treatment of the subject, the Virgin is larger than the other figures. Angels broadcast the news of Christ's coming and the prospect of Peace on Earth; the devils scatter.

Page 17

The Virgin and Child in a Landscape
Attributed to Jan Provoost
(living 1491; died 1529)
The mother and child sit in the countryside, surrounded by plants and flowers. Jesus is playing with a whirligig, a toy with a spinning top. To his left is a pot of carnations, which was probably used to symbolize his suffering and his death on the Cross.

Pages 18 and 19

Christ Glorified in Heaven
Fra Angelico
(active 1417; died 1455)
See the entry for the cover and jacket flaps.

Page 20

The Adoration of the Kings
Jan Brueghel the Elder
(1568-1625)
Brueghel's paintings are full of lively detail, such as the crowd of onlookers in the foreground of this painting, the figures on the bank of the river in the background and Joseph's wood-working tools in the lower right corner.

Page 23

Seraphim, Cherubim and Adoring Angels
Jacopo di Cione
(active about 1362; died 1398/1400)
This was one of two panels of adoring angels that formed part of the altarpiece of a church in Florence (see *The Nativity and the Annunciation*, page 11).

Page 24

The Rest on the Flight into Egypt
Master of the Female Half-Lengths
(16th century)
The Holy Family is shown resting and refreshing themselves on their journey into Egypt to escape Herod. In the background, a man is at work in the field of corn that grew miraculously overnight to mislead Herod's soldiers.

Page 27

A Scene on the Ice near a Town
Hendrick Avercamp
(1585-1634)
The figures skating, riding in hand-drawn sleighs, and playing *Kolf* (an early version of golf) on the frozen river could be from drawings and sketches made from life, although the town may be imaginary.

Page 29

A Winter Scene
Isack van Ostade
(1621-49)
The details of the frozen landscape and of the figures going about their daily lives highlight the effects of winter in the countryside. The man struggling over the bridge with his firewood, and the man guiding his horse and sleigh onto the bank are contrasted with the pleasure of the child who is waiting to go on the ice.

Page 31

The Adoration of the Shepherds
Louis (?) le Nain
(about 1593-1648)
Le Nain painted many pictures of ordinary country people. Here, the barefoot man kneeling with his back to us is a shepherd. The angels look like peasant children, with their tousled hair and curious glances.

Page 32

The Adoration of the Shepherds
Nicolas Poussin
(about 1594-1665)
In this painting the Christian scene of the adoration contains many classical allusions in the ruins behind the Holy Family and the style of dress of the figures. The ruins and the new-born child symbolize the ending of an era with the birth of Christ.

Page 34

The Adoration of the Magi
Carlo Dolci
(1616-86)
One of the most famous painters of his day, Dolci painted many religious pictures. Here the three richly dressed kings kneel before Mary in the dark stable to offer their gifts to Jesus.

Page 36

Peasants Merry-making Before a Country House
Lucas van Uden (1595-1672) and David Teniers the Younger (1610-90)
Both the painters lived in Antwerp and worked together on a number of paintings. The landscape was painted by van Uden and the people merry-making in the foreground by David Teniers, who is well known for his scenes of country life.

Page 38

A Winter Landscape
Caspar David Friedrich
(1774-1840)
This German artist often painted landscapes with a symbolic meaning. Here the message is one of hope: the man has thrown away his crutches and sits against a rock with his hands raised in prayer.

Page 41

A Concert
Lorenzo Costa
(1459/60-1535)
This was probably one of a series of paintings of singers with different musical instruments. Artists in Costa's time were interested in conveying the idea of sound, in this case singing, and demonstrating their skill in showing expressions on people's faces (see the angels in Piero della Francesca's *Nativity*, page 9).

Hark! The Herald Angels Sing
© 1993 Frances Lincoln Limited

Picture index
© 1993 Frances Lincoln Limited

Music arrangements
© 1993 Barrie Carson Turner
Burgate, Diss, Norfolk, IP22 1QG

All illustrations reproduced by courtesy of the Trustees, The National Gallery, London.

First published in Great Britain in 1993 by Frances Lincoln Limited, Apollo Works
5 Charlton Kings Road, London NW5 2SB

British Library Cataloguing in Publication Data available on request

ISBN 0-7112-0814-X

Set in Baskerville
Printed and bound in Hong Kong

Designed by Patricia Howes

9 8 7 6 5 4 3 2 1

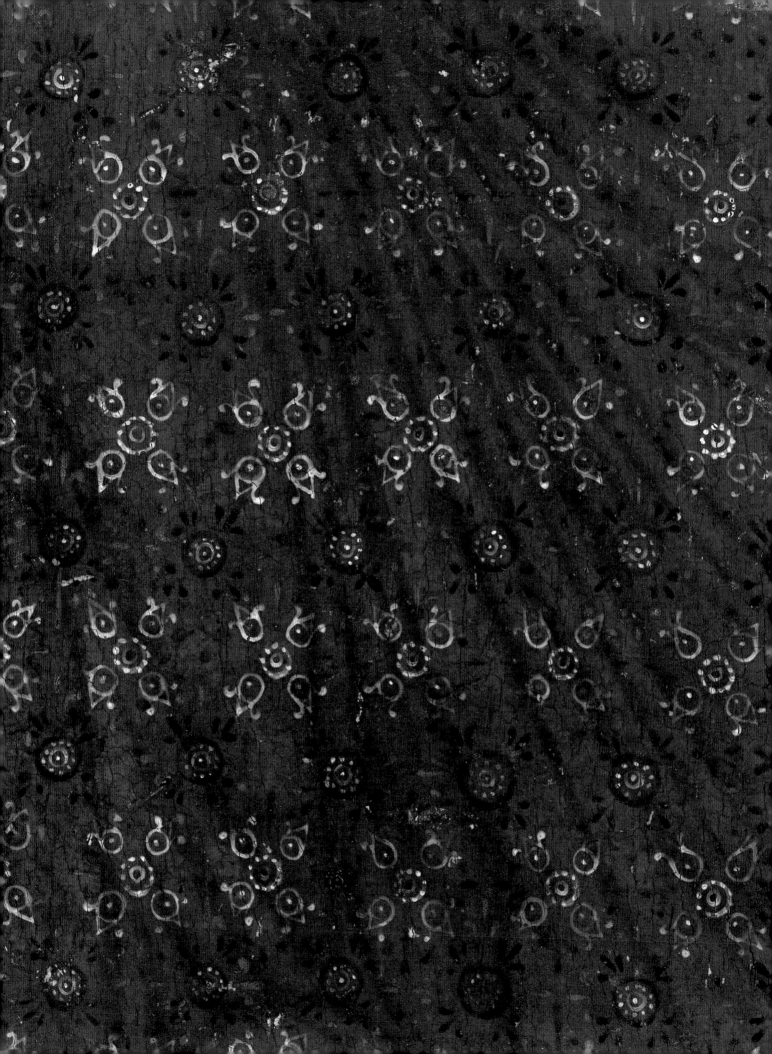